IMAGES
of America

BOYLSTON

IMAGES
of America

BOYLSTON

William O. Dupuis

ARCADIA
PUBLISHING

Copyright © 2000 by William O. Dupuis
ISBN 978-1-5316-0220-8

Published by Arcadia Publishing
Charleston, South Carolina

Library of Congress Catalog Card Number: 2008943467

For all general information contact Arcadia Publishing at:
Telephone 843-853-2070
Fax 843-853-0044
E-mail sales@arcadiapublishing.com
For customer service and orders:
Toll-Free 1-888-313-2665

Visit us on the Internet at www.arcadiapublishing.com

Dedicated to Friends Past and Present

Cover: This 1900 winter scene of Boylston center typifies the very nature of the town. On the left is the original Center Store and to the right is the 1830 Town Hall.

Old time Boylston is well depicted in this 1903 photo. An unidentified farmer with his hay wagon is leading his oxen back to the barn.

CONTENTS

ACKNOWLEDGMENTS

A work such as this demands the efforts and talents of many people. First and foremost, my sincerest gratitude goes out to the wonderful staff of the Boylston Historical Society Museum: Frederick Brown, Judy Haynes, Betty Thomas, and Norm French. Without their total commitment and unswerving support, not a page of this book would have ever seen a press.

To the many and mostly unknown photographers whose work graces these pages, I offer my thanks. Unbeknownst to them, they left behind a treasury of images that allows us to see into past ages of this community.

To past historians of Boylston, like Matthew Davenport and George L. Wright, whose writings form the foundation of our understanding of this area's past, I salute you! Their research allows us to put names to faces, events to buildings, and flesh to the bare bones of history.

To the children of Boylston, whose curiosity about their town's past continues to inspire those of us who struggle to preserve our heritage. They are a constant source of encouragement and motivation.

To the senior citizens whose anecdotes help us to better appreciate what life was like here "in the good old days!" We are grateful for your interest and valuable memories.

To the Boylston Historical Society for allowing me to freely peruse their extensive photo collection and for permission to use whatever I wanted. All photos are from the society's collection unless otherwise indicated.

To those who allowed me to use their private photos, including Mrs. Ruth Coyle, St. Mary of the Hills Church, Mary Hehir, The Huntington Library of San Marino, California, Kenneth Wagner, and Roger Wentzell for his photos of the Model Dairy, I give sincere gratitude. To friends whose encouragement was truly inspirational, I offer my undying indebtedness.

INTRODUCTION

A 19th-century Boylston admirer described the community as "the heart of the heart of the Commonwealth," a comment which must have sent a shiver through the inhabitants of nearby Worcester. Boylston began its existence as a part of two neighboring communities: Lancaster to the north and Shrewsbury to the southeast. Although not blessed with the richest soil for agriculture, the land and streams teemed with wildlife. From the very beginning agriculture was the principal occupation of the early settlers, but there were also enough mill keepers, blacksmiths, and tavern keepers to furnish the farmers with vital services. Settled around 1722 in the valley of the Nashua River, Boylston has become, in the 20th century, a bedroom town that keeps much of its traditional rural charm, yet affords easy access to the centers of industry, technology, and the arts

By 1730, over 20 families had settled in the area, with more arriving every year. In 1742, the inhabitants of the bottom two-thirds petitioned the mother town of Shrewsbury to be allowed to seek township status. The move was opposed and received a negative vote in the General Court; however, the area was allowed to become a Precinct of Shrewsbury with a modicum of independence. The Precinct fielded a company of Minutemen at the alarm of 1775 and sent a respectable number of volunteers to the Continental Army. The first minister, Reverend Ebenezer Morse, became the leader of a sizable Tory opposition for which he was forcibly removed from his pulpit.

In 1786, township status was finally approved and the town took the name of a prominent commercial family in Boston. Within a short time, the top third was also joined to the new community. However, by 1808, the western section of Boylston decided to secede from the main community and became the town of West Boylston. In 1848, John B. Gough, the Temperance lecturer who would become internationally famous and bring his message of abstinence to nine million people, built a home in Boylston. He called it "Hillside" and it became a mecca for social reformers, politicians, clergymen, artists, and the temperance faithful.

An industrial center began to take shape along the banks of the Nashua. Settled originally by the Sawyer family, it was the site of a sawmill, gristmill, clothier mill, fuller mill, oil mill, a blacksmith shop, and was surrounded by homes, farms, a store, a church, and a school. By 1862, the Lancaster Mill Corporation established a textile mill at the site, which by then was called Sawyer's Mills. The plant employed 125 people, mostly immigrant Irish, French Canadian, and German. It processed over a million pounds of cotton yarn per year.

However, farming continued to be the main source of employment. Farmers grew a variety

7

of grain, vegetables, and fruit. The town was famous for its apple orchards, the fine cider it produced, and animal husbandry. Nevertheless, in the late 1890s, the need for fresh water by Boston caused the building of the Wachusett Reservoir. Boylston lost almost 2,800 acres of land, its industrial center, homes, farms, a store, post office, schools, and a church. Some predicted the demise of the town. Despite the loss, or perhaps because of it, the hardy inhabitants struggled back and restructured their community.

In this century, the Great War interrupted the quiet life of the town and forty of its sons and daughters marched off to war. Fortunately all returned safely. The Depression took its toll and Prohibition spawned a surprising number of homemade stills. In the 1920s a trolley track ran from north to south through the town, linking it with Worcester. It allowed many immigrant workers the opportunity to leave the urban sprawl and move to a gentler setting while still working in the city. Ninety men and women saw service in World War II. Sadly, three of Boylston's sons never returned. However, the war brought significant changes to the town. More families began to build homes and slowly but surely the farms disappeared and the character of the town changed forever.

The photos in this book are meant not only to reflect our past, but also to motivate us to ponder the future. We are, after all, what we have been. Boylston's future will hopefully always contain the characteristics of its earlier age—tranquillity, peace, and pride.

One

SPACES AND PLACES

A photo of the fireplace in the Bartlett house, also known as Strawberry Hill Farm, was taken in the early 1900s. The house itself was built c. 1750. Note the fine scrollwork around the mantle, and the Dutch ovens to the left.

Before 1900, the Nashua River meandered through the western section of town. The young people who frequented it during the summer called this spot the "Black Rock Swimming Hole." The photo was taken from the Scar Hill Bridge.

N. RES. - BOYLSTON
OCT. 28, 1896

744

This is what you would have seen if you rode into the center of Sawyer's Mills in 1896. At the left is the store and post office. At the right is the Sawyer homestead occupied by the superintendent of the textile mill. Up the street was the Catholic chapel. For a time, Sawyer's Mills rivaled Boylston Center as the hub of the town.

Thomas Cunningham was an enterprising Scotsman who created a picnic grove on his land, which abutted the Nashua River, around the time of the Civil War. This c. 1880 photo shows the area where young men from the area canoed on Sunday afternoons to court young women.

The Avenue of Pines led to the cemetery on Scar Hill Road. The trees had been planted around the time of the Civil War. This beautiful avenue was totally destroyed by the hurricane of September 1938.

This house was formerly a wheelwright shop located at the northern end of the old cemetery. It was purchased by Levi L. Flagg, moved to the knoll westerly of the cemetery, and changed into a private dwelling. It was later owned by the Maynard family. The photo dates to *c*. 1890.

This 1886 photo shows the home of Levi Lincoln Flagg. The original house burned in the early 1800s and was rebuilt by Mr. Flagg. It was located on Route 140 near the site of the present Dragon 88 Restaurant.

Both of these photos are of the same little girl, Bertha Annie Knight (b. 1889). It's February, 1900 and she is out for a sleigh ride. The photo was taken in front of the Boyden house on the common. With the caption "Did I take out my slide?" we see Miss Knight all bundled up in fur parked in front of the town hall. Both photos were taken from postcards sent by Bertha to her father, Charles Knight, who was in Clinton Hospital at the time.

This destroyed roadway is the result of the overflowing of French Brook in 1927. This photo was taken on Route 70 near Main Street Circle. One of the persons in the picture is Gus Hakala.

In the wake of severe rains in 1927, French Brook burst its banks and moved across the present Route 70. The telephone pole marks the roadway. All that remains is the trolley track, which looks like a suspended bridge.

"The Pines" was built by Revolutionary War Veteran Deacon Jonathan Bond in c. 1757 on the corner of Main Street and Sanatorium Road. John Gough lived here while his home was being built in 1848. It is believed that it was subsequently used as the home for the senior farmhand at Hillside.

This is an 1886 photo of the Strawberry Hill Farm, owned by the Bartlett family, and built between 1743 and 1755. The stones for the building of the library were quarried at the site.

At the place where French Brook crossed the present Main Street Circle was a 40-foot falls called Dinner Pail Falls. This *c.* 1910 photo shows Boylston's answer to Niagara Falls! It is said that a schoolgirl lost her lunch pail down the falls thus giving it its name.

This is the stump of the largest chestnut tree in the area. The tree grew on the property of Levi Lincoln Flagg. When it was taken down *c.* 1880, it yielded 15 cords of wood. The stump itself lasted until 1940 when it was taken apart for firewood. Shown here are Jennie and Russell Flagg.

The infamous 1938 hurricane brought death and destruction to the Northeast. In the center of Boylston, this large tree was uprooted, and a telephone pole left at an angle in front of the library.

The 1938 hurricane also toppled trees in the old cemetery, and even toppled stones.

The Solomon Houghton house was built before 1760 at what is now 330 Linden Street. Houghton was a prominent Tory during the Revolutionary War and was pursued by Colonial officials for distributing counterfeit currency. He hid in a cave in the East Woods and later escaped to Nova Scotia.

This was originally the Daniel Hastings place, settled by him in 1725. He came with his wife on horseback from Watertown, a trip that took several days. His son David inherited the place, and after his death, it reverted to his widow. She later married A.V.R. Prouty. This is an 1886 print.

Before the advent of the Wachusett Reservoir, the town maintained several bridges across the Nashua River, including this one at the end of Scar Hill Road. This 1900 photo shows the bridge being inundated as Wachusett was being filled.

Immigrant labor was imported to build the Wachusett Reservoir. This c. 1896 photo shows workers near the Clinton line preparing the water basin for the coming of the waters. Amazingly, all of the labor was done by hand.

A view down Central Street taken around 1890 shows some of the early homes and farms. The home on the far left is 246 Central Street. It was originally built around 1730, and owned by Daniel Hastings.

This bucolic scene of pasture and farms was taken in the late 1800s from Davenport Hill, in the western section of town.

Two

ALL WORK
AND NO PLAY

Boylston has had a long theatrical history. Seven local actors in this turn-of-the-century photo are seated on the stage in the old town hall, resplendent in their costumes. Shown are, from left to right, Mrs. George Longley, Mrs. Burtis Garfield, Mrs. Loring Reed, Miss Mabel Flagg, Mrs. Charles S. Knight, ? Christianson, and Elaine Mann. Boylston continues to supply fine actors, including Jean Louisa Kelly of movie and TV fame.

These Fourth of July (1922) revelers are milling about in front of a food booth sponsored by the Boylston Men's Club. Three of the young women are Anna and Kathleen Knight, and Dorothy Butterfield.

Harry Souci, at the left in the white tuxedo, directed this 1940 Musical Review. Souci, a former chorus boy in the Ziegfeld Follies, began variety reviews in 1930 and was producer, choreographer, and musical director. At the right, the woman in the black gown is Florence Maynard, who often assisted Souci. Lady Liberty is Aldine Fuller Bemis.

24

The Alabama Minstrel Troupe

WILL GIVE A

MINSTREL SHOW

IN TOWN HALL, BOYLSTON
Friday Evening, Dec. 10, '15

Interlocutor—CHARLES KNIGHT
End Men
George Bell   Chester Shattuck
      Herbert French   Richard Flagg
Chorus
Fred Hall   Peter Stewart   Orrin Weston
Harold French   Robert Andrews   Fred Stark
Lloyd Lent   Jack Hakala   Elmer Garfield
                       Fred Longley
Pianist—Harry Souci

PROGRAM

OPENING CHORUS......"All Aboard for Dixie Land"
            "Somebody Knows"
            "Little Spark of Love still Burning"
SOLO.........................."Alabama Jubilee"
            Mr. Harold French
SOLO.................."Over the Hills to Mary"
            Mr. Peter Stewart
SOLO.................."Down in Bom Bombay"
            Mr. Robert Andrews
DUET............ "When I Dream of Old Erin"
      Mr. Lloyd Lent and Mr. Peter Stewart
SOLO............ .... "Sweet Adair"
            Mr. Fred Stark
SOLO.................."The Little Grey Mother"
            Mr. Lloyd Lent
SOLO.................."Back Home in Tennessee"
            Mr. Jack Hakala
SOLO......... "It's nice fo get up in the Morning"
            Mr. Peter Stewart
END SONG.................."Kentucky Home"
            Mr George Bell
END SONG...................."Jane Dear"

Boylston's "Alabama Minstrel Troupe" gave a performance on December 10, 1915. The program consisted of music and humorous patter.

The newly formed Men's Club of Boylston began producing annual minstrel shows. This cast, c. 1923, is pictured in front of the stone fireplace in the basement of the Town House. The gentleman in the back row with the goatee is Charles Knight, who served as the interlocutor for this production. The other cast members are not identified.

Minstrel shows were popular in Boylston during the first several decades of the 20th century. Early shows were produced by the Dramatic Club founded in 1901, and later by the Men's Club. The members of this 1915 production include, from left to right, George Ball; Fred Shattuck; Harry Souci, and Charles Knight in drag; Robert Flagg; and Herbert French.

A bazaar was held to benefit the newly formed Men's Club in May, 1922, on the second floor of the town hall. The couple at the left is holding a sign that reads "DONATED." This could be a kissing booth with two lovely vendors just waiting for customers, but somehow that is doubtful! Incidentally, the little girl seated at the left is Barbara Knight.

This 1902 photo shows the cast of *The Old Folks Concert*. The cast includes the following, from left to right: (front row) Miss E. Burnett Tucker, and Charles Knight; (second row) Mrs. Munson Flagg, Abbie Flagg, Mrs. Loring Reed, Dorothy Garfield, Mrs. Charles Knight, Mrs. James Woods, Mrs. George Shattuck, Mrs. Burtis Garfield, Mrs. John Davis, Carrie Rice, and Mrs. Andrew Stanhope; (third row) ? Christianson, Henrietta Andrews, Harold French, Mrs. Charles Bray, Amy Garfield, Mrs. Joseph Garfield, Mrs. Calvin Andrews, Mrs. Levi Longley, and Mrs. George Dodge; (fourth row) Samuel Butterfield, Fred Hall, Charles Bray, George Keogh, Fred Stark, Chester Bartlett, Rev. George Dodge, Charles C. Bray, and Alonzo Ball.

THE OPERETTA

— OF —

GOLDEN HAIR <small>AND</small> THREE BEARS

WILL BE GIVEN IN THE

TOWN HALL BOYLSTON,

Monday Evening, Oct. 14, 1889.

Under the direction of Mrs. H. M. Andrews.

PERSONATIONS.

Golden Hair,	Sybil H. Flagg
Woodland Queen,	Lula M. Bray
Faithful,	Grace D. Lovett
Lightfoot,	Maud O. Webber
Frailty,	Ida F. Bates
Airy,	Lizzie H. Bray
Will-O'-The-Wisp,	Esther M. Reed
Woodland Maiden,	Daisy E. Flagg
Bard,	Charles C. Bray
Big Bruin,	Calvin H. Andrews
Mammy Muff.	Charles I. Barnes
Tiny Cub,	Robbie B. Andrews

Chorus of Forest Children.

Pianist, Miss Mamie E. Andrews.

Admission 20 cents.   Children 10 cents.

The proceeds to be given for purchasing a piano for the Town Hall.

Sanford & Davis Prt. & From USA, Worcester, Mass.

This flier advertised the operetta *Golden Hair and the Three Bears*, which was performed in 1889 by a group of talented Boylstonians.

The Boylston Grange was founded in 1883 to provide both practical advice to farmers and a source of entertainment. This bevy of beauties had just been inducted into the Flora Team, c. 1910. Shown are, from left to right, the following: (front row) June Glynn, Grace Monigle, Mrs. George Taylor, Mrs. Robert Andrews, Mrs. Frank Hopkins, Annie Benson, and Elizabeth Blackwell; (back row) Mrs. Walter Devoe, Mrs. Harry Butterfield, Mrs. Burtis Garfield, Mrs. Charles Knight, Mrs. Joseph Garfield, Tillie Voss, and Mrs. George Brousseau.

The 1915 production of *The Girls of 1776* was a continuation of a 35-year dramatic tradition in Boylston. Pictured here at the extreme left are, from left to right, as follows: (front row) Mrs. Burtis Garfield, others unknown; (middle row) Mrs. Orrin Weston; (back row) Mrs. Howard Shattuck, Goldie Benson, Mary Keogh, Mrs. Charles Knight, Kate Taylor, Mrs. Elmer Durrell, Annie Tollman, Grace Poor, Mrs. Romeo Sweet, and Mrs. George Longley.

The Boylston Brass Band was founded in 1874 to play at parades and social events. This c. 1890 photo was taken on the side of the Center School. Shown are, from left to right, the following: (front row) Fred Stark, Robert Andrews, Fred Longley, and Cornelius Longley; (back row) George Vickery, Will Carney, Philip Bigelow, James Longley, one unknown person, Homer Clark, Clarence Allen, Munson Flagg, Fay Bennett, M. Brigham, Richard Flagg, Allard Ball, one unknown person, Levi Longley, and Gus Voss.

A dramatic production sponsored by the Boylston Drama Club and presented on the stage of the town hall dates from c. 1910. It appears to have been an ethnic piece judging from the costumes of the actors. Here are, from left to right, Maude Shattuck, William Garfield, Fred Stark, Carl Malberg, Amy Kendall, George Keogh, Mabel Flagg, James Longley, Mary Kimball, Richard Flagg, Gertrude Franklin, John Kimball, Grace Monigle, Robert Andrews, and Miss Christianson.

This appears to be an early version of a toga party, but it's really a patriotic pageant presented in 1919. The participants posing on the steps of the Boylston Public Library are, from left to right, Maude Hazard, Louise Allen, Dorothy Garfield, Rebecca ?, Grace Tollman, Mrs. Prouty, Bertha Garfield, one unknown person, Mrs. Doyle, and Mrs. Charles Knight.

On September 13, 1919, Boylston sponsored a Welcome Home Day for returning World War I veterans. Included was a band concert, the unveiling of the Honor Roll, and a patriotic pageant, "America, Yesterday and Today" with 100 citizens taking part. These Boylston belles are posing in front of the library and are, from left to right, Hazel Durrell, Grace Mentzer, Harriet Longley, Marion Stark, Verna Dowd, Marion Lovell, Rosabell Hastings, and Verna Hager.

Doing some serious digging in 1922, these members of the Men's Club are hard at work building their new clubhouse. The members shown are, from left to right, the following: Gus Hakala, Jack Maynard, one unknown member, Harry Lovell, and Charles Knight.

In early 1923, the interior of the new Men's Club was taking shape. This is a view of the auditorium.

Arthur Peterson is having a grand time driving this Cletrac tractor in 1922 as part of the building of the Men's Club, now known as the Town House. Close to 90% of the men in Boylston belonged to the new club. Only one topic was taboo—politics! They were smart men!

The building to house the Boylston Men's Club was built in 1922. It was used for social events until 1938 when the town purchased it.

In the 1930s, Kate Taylor converted the old barn next to the Center Store into a restaurant with the appropriate name, "The Red Barn Grain Bin." This photo taken in the early 1940s shows the entrance to the eatery, which was popular not only with the locals but with people from Clinton and Worcester.

This late 1930s picture shows the interior of the Red Barn Grain Bin. Much of the original barn was used as part of the décor. This scene was used as a postcard advertising the restaurant.

This second photo of the interior of the Red Barn was taken around 1930 and shows a homey and inviting atmosphere.

A small area to the rear of the Red Barn Grain Bin was used in the summer months allowing patrons to dine outside amidst flowers and bushes. Nobody ever said Boylston did not have class.

The focal point of this 1900 winter scene on the common is the outdoor privy adjacent to the town hall building. The caption, "The Actor's Retreat," was a humorous comment made on the postcard that was sent to Charles Knight, who was in the hospital at the time. Mr. Knight was a perennial actor in most of Boylston's theatrical productions.

Two

WAR AND PARADES

The Red Barn Grain Bin created this float for the 1936 Sesquicentennial Celebration. It features a replica of the restaurant surrounded by some lovely women who were waitresses at the eatery. In front are Edith Anderson, Elizabeth Brigham, and June Shattuck. In the back are Miss Askalis and Helen Lund. John Woods is the driver.

Private John Roberts, son of a French Canadian widow, was the first Boylston man to enlist in the Civil War. He joined the 2nd Massachusetts Volunteers and saw action in North Carolina and Virginia. John was killed at the Battle of Cedar Mountain, Virginia, at the age of 25, and was the first man from Boylston to give his life in this conflict.

J. Henry Flagg enlisted in the 5th Massachusetts Volunteers in 1862. He served as both an artilleryman and a drummer. In private life, he was a grocery clerk. This photo dates to c. 1862.

John W. Partridge enlisted in the 25th Massachusetts Volunteers in 1861. He was a teacher in Boylston and he had joined the army along with a fellow teacher and several former students. He was captured at New Berne, North Carolina, on February 1, 1864. He was at first believed killed, but it soon became evident that he had been captured. He was sent to the infamous Andersonville Prison in Georgia, where he died of dysentery and malnutrition on April 12, 1864.

First Lieutenant J. Emerson Holbrook enlisted in the 25th Massachusetts Volunteers at the age of 20. He was later attached to the Independent Battalion of Ohio Cavalry where he received his commission. He was discharged in 1864 and was the only Boylston man to be commissioned an officer during the Civil War.

In August 1886, the town celebrated its centennial with several days of parades, concerts, and speeches. This photo shows the old common between the present Route 70 and School Street. The arch reads "Dear to the Heart are the Scenes of Childhood." The woman, her son, and the carriage in the background are touching signs of a bygone era.

This 1886 centennial photo shows in the background the Boyden House decorated with bunting. The picture was taken from an early bandstand on the new common.

The two venerable men pictured here
are Charles Webber (left) and Lyman
Walker. Mr. Walker served in the
Civil War with the 24th Massachusetts
Volunteers. This *c.* 1919 photo shows
these veterans wearing the uniform of
the Grand Army of the Republic.

Charles Newell was the father of
the Boylston family of that name.
He served in the Spanish-American
War in 1898 as chief quartermaster
aboard the USS *Catskill*. He is
pictured here in his naval uniform.

Among Boylston's young men who served in World War I was H. Lloyd Brigham pictured in this 1918 photo. He served with the 321st Infantry Regiment in France. He was hit with poison gas in April 1918, and was awarded the Purple Heart. Lloyd returned home where he joined the postal service. He was an avid historian who researched Boylston family histories.

This 1919 photo shows three friends from Boylston on their return from France to America, having served in the American Expeditionary Force. Shown from left to right are Elmer Garfield, Fred Christiensen, and H. Lloyd Brigham.

Reception

Given by

CITIZENS of BOYLSTON

to her

Soldier Boys

Oct. 20th, 1917

Menu

Escalloped Oysters

Cold Meat   Potato Salad

Rolls

Celery   Pickles

Pie

Ice Cream   Cake   Fruit

Coffee

Stobbs Press, 25 Foster St., Worcester Mass.

This menu, including escalloped oysters, is for the "Reception for Soldier Boys" (October 20, 1917), given in honor of young men departing for service in World War I.

A doll carriage parade in the 1920s featured one carriage on the right covered in flowers. Unfortunately, there is no way to know if it won first prize.

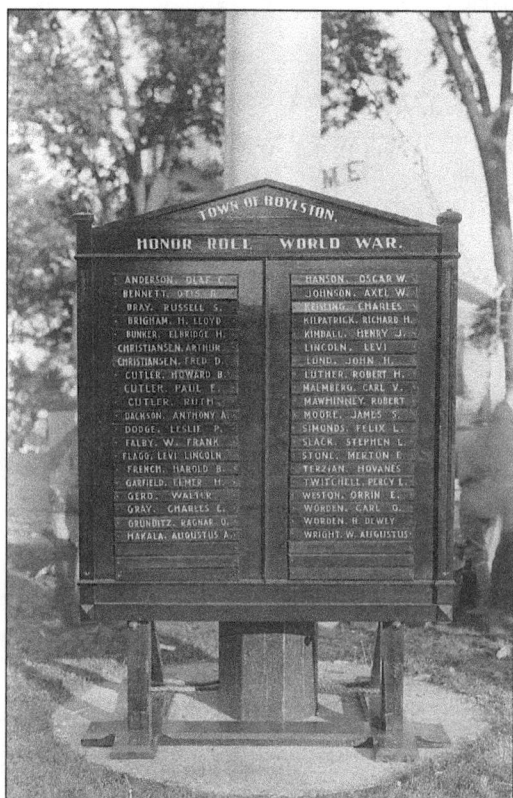

TOWN OF BOYLSTON.

HONOR ROLL   WORLD WAR.

ANDERSON, OLAF C.	HANSON, OSCAR W.
BENNETT, OTIS L.	JOHNSON, AXEL W.
BRAY, RUSSELL S.	KEISLING, CHARLES
BRIGHAM, H. LLOYD	KILPATRICK, RICHARD H.
BUNKER, ELBRIDGE H.	KIMBALL, HENRY J.
CHRISTIANSEN, ARTHUR	LINCOLN, LEVI
CHRISTIANSEN, FRED D.	LUND, JOHN H.
CUTLER, HOWARD B.	LUTHER, ROBERT H.
CUTLER, PAUL E.	MALMBERG, CARL V.
CUTLER, RUTH	MAWHINNEY, ROBERT
DACKSON, ANTHONY A.	MOORE, JAMES S.
DODGE, LESLIE P.	SIMONDS, FELIX L.
FALBY, W. FRANK	SLACK, STEPHEN L.
FLAGG, LEVI LINCOLN	STONE, MERTON E.
FRENCH, HAROLD B.	TERZIAN, HOVANES
GARFIELD, ELMER M.	TWITCHELL, PERCY L.
GERD, WALTER	WESTON, ORRIN E.
GRAY, CHARLES E.	WORDEN, CARL O.
GRUNDITZ, RAGNAR O.	WORDEN, H. DEWEY
HAKALA, AUGUSTUS A.	WRIGHT, W. AUGUSTUS

The names of 39 men and one woman are listed on this World War I Honor Roll, which was dedicated in September 1919. It was erected at the base of the flagpole on the new common.

The Morningdale Ladies Aid entered this float in the 1936 Sesquicentennial Parade. Members working on a quilt are, from left to right, Mary E. Hager, Mrs. Burnett, Mrs. Alfred Brousseau, Mrs. Butterfield, and Mrs. Elsie Nylen. An ancient spinning wheel is to the left.

This 1936 Sesquicentennial float features Boylston Grange members on a wagon filled with hay. The participants are not identified.

100 UNITED STATES OF AMERICA
OFFICE OF PRICE ADMINISTRATION 100

186145 G

RATION COUPON
FOR
ONE HUNDRED
POINTS
PROCESSED FOODS
100 OPA Form R-1326 ☆ GPO 16—34716-1 100

100 UNITED STATES OF AMERICA
OFFICE OF PRICE ADMINISTRATION

186146 G

RATION COUPON
FOR
ONE HUNDRED
POINTS
PROCESSED FOODS
100 OPA Form R-1326 ☆ GPO 16—34716-1

100 UNITED STATES OF AMERICA
OFFICE OF PRICE ADMINISTRATION 100

186147 G

RATION COUPON
FOR
ONE HUNDRED
POINTS
PROCESSED FOODS
100 OPA Form R-1326 ☆ GPO 16—34716-1 100

100 UNITED STATES OF AMERICA
OFFICE OF PRICE ADMINISTRATION

186148 G

RATION COUPON
FOR
ONE HUNDRED
POINTS
PROCESSED FOODS
100 OPA Form R-1326 ☆ GPO 16—34716-1

100 UNITED STATES OF AMERICA
OFFICE OF PRICE ADMINISTRATION 100

186149 G

RATION COUPON
FOR
ONE HUNDRED
POINTS
PROCESSED FOODS
100 OPA Form R-1326 ☆ GPO 16—34716-1 100

100 UNITED STATES OF AMERICA
OFFICE OF PRICE ADMINISTRATION

186150 G

RATION COUPON
FOR
ONE HUNDRED
POINTS
PROCESSED FOODS
100 OPA Form R-1326 ☆ GPO 16—34716-1

These are samples of World War II ration coupons for processed food.

Marion V. Donaldson was the first Boylston woman to be commissioned in the Women's Army Corps. She was made a 2nd Lieutenant in 1942. When she was finally separated from the Army, she had attained the rank of major. In addition to her military career, Major Donaldson was also employed by the American Red Cross and was a teacher for the YMCA. (Ruth Coyle photo.)

Private William H. Brown was one of three Boylston men who lost their lives during World War II. He was killed in action on April 17, 1945, on Monterumici, near Florence, Italy. He was awarded a Bronze Star for bravery in this action. He lies in the Military Cemetery in Florence. William was 28 years old at his death.

47

In 1937, the town erected a memorial to all the men and women who had served their country during all of its wars. It is perched atop a small mound overlooking the new common and is the center of Memorial Day activities. True to a long standing Boylston tradition, years of wrangling passed before the memorial was built.

Four

GOLDEN RULE DAYS

The town sponsored a high school class at the old town hall building with nearly 60 students of all ages attending around 1852.

A full view of the East, or Brick, School was taken c. 1890. The students and their teacher are posing for the camera. Note the disparity of ages among the students. It is likely that the teacher is the woman on the far left with an apron. When the building was dismantled, the brick (covered by stucco) was used to build the Fuller house on Main Street.

This is the East School located on Central Street. Built in 1850, it was one of six one-room schoolhouses that dotted Boylston's landscape. Photographed in 1900, these scholars are, from left to right, as follows: (bottom row) Lloyd Brigham, Harry Winchester, Bertha Winchester, Lena Wright, and Maude Wright; (second row) Clifford Winchester, Howard Cutler, Leon Winchester, and Frank Falbey; (top row) Lee Hastings, Earl Hastings, Charlotte Brigham, Lillian Falbey, and Walter Brigham. The teacher is Miss Bailey.

The Center School was built in 1850 and was in use until 1904. It sat on the site of the present public library. By actual count, 47 different types of textbooks were in use, many of them out of date.

The Sawyer's Mills Schoolhouse was built in 1851. This fine schoolhouse has the distinction of holding the first Catholic mass in Boylston. It served the children of the mill workers and of the farmers in the immediate area. Note the "Tom Sawyer" type picket fence in front of it.

The Northeast Schoolhouse was built in 1809 on the so-called Clinton Road. It is often referred to as "The Six Nations" School because it was attended by the children of many of the immigrants who lived in that section of town. It continued to serve the children of Boylston until 1899, when it was taken by the Commonwealth for the building of the Wachusett Reservoir.

A truly great school photo, this was probably taken at the Six Nations School in the 1880s. No one is identified, but the teacher is clearly in the center. Note the diverse ages of students in this one-room school, and how the children are dressed. Three of the boys are barefoot and all have short haircuts.

The Northeast School had one of Boylston's most famous teachers, Dr. Samuel Brigham, who was an accomplished writer and educator. This photo dates to c. 1880.

The South School was located at the corner of what is now Route 140 and Sewall Street. Built in 1851, it was the second schoolhouse at that site. This c. 1900 photo shows a neat and tidy schoolhouse.

The graduating class of 1942 is pictured in front of the Consolidated School. Shown are, from left to right, as follows: (front row) Norman French, Allyn Kimball, Donald Whalen, Charlie Gray, one unknown student, and Clayton Fuller; (second row) Elsie Marderosian, Margie Rogers, Helen Twitchell, Carolyn Danforth, Alice Chiarelli, Sally Ann Hakala, Noleine Kelleher, and one unknown student; (third row) Ms. Corridan, Viola Chiarelli, (possibly) Eleanor Slack, Helen Johnson, Alice Chiarelli, Ardelle Newell, and Martha Fuller; (fourth row) Principal Farnum, Norma Hakala, Margaret McLean, Shirley Reed, Katherine Lucia, June Shattuck, one unknown student, and Dana Adams; (fifth row) Jackie Durkin, Jack Stark, Daniel McDougald, Bobbie Johnson, and Bob Jennison.

It was at the Consolidated School in 1908 that the Boylston Graduates Association was founded. It is the oldest continuing eighth grade association that continues in the nation.

In 1904, the one-room schoolhouses were abolished. The brand new Consolidated School was built where the tennis courts are presently located in Boylston center. The carriages or barges pictured here were used to transport students to areas beyond the center. In the winter months, sleighs were used. Today, some children do not like to travel on buses!

These students at the Consolidated School were photographed in September 1931. No one is identified. The Consolidated School was in operation until 1957. when the present Boylston Elementary School replaced it.

The class of 1926 photographed on the new common include, from left to right, the following: (first row) Ethel Johnson, Elva Ekblom, Sarah Stearns, Nellie ?, Dorothy Symonds, Margaret Adams, and Emma Chiarelli; (second row) Walter Rease, Doris Durrell, Kathy Knight, Dinah Levine, Elmer Brown, and Harold Scott; (third row) Joe Carroll, Jimmy Jeffrey, Howard Bunker, Robert Brown, David Brigham, and Arthur Wheeler.

This photo of the fifth and sixth grades of the Consolidated School was taken c. 1907. Shown are, from left to right, the following: (front row) Myra Bennett, Dewey Warden, Dorothy Garfield, Myra Young, Marian Brigham, Grace Murphy, and Gertrude Flagg; (middle row) Paul Cutler, Lena Wright, John Hakala, Eubert Mellaly, Augustus Hakala, Walter Gero, and David Sohlstrom; (back row) Bertha Walker, Henrietta Gould, Maude Wright, Statia Sanders, Goldie Prouty, and Warren Wright.

Five

IT TRAVELS HOW FAST?

The Worcester & Clinton Trolley line was organized in 1898, ran through Morningdale, Boylston center, and Clinton, and ended up in Fitchburg. This 1910 photo shows a suburban car leaving Worcester for Boylston. On certain sections of the line, it attained speeds of 45 to 50 miles an hour!

"Sleigh bells ring . . ." in this winter wonderland in Boylston Center sometime around 1910. The young woman in the sleigh sports a fur hat and a fur lap rug. Looking carefully, the trolley tracks are visible on the side of the road. Somehow, this manner of transportation is more romantic and appealing.

Frank Bannister (1870–19??) and his dog are pictured in his convertible buggy parked in front of the brick tavern carriage house on Main Street, c. 1900.

The Barre-Paxton-Worcester Stagecoach is captured in this 1915 photo. Women were seated in the coach while the men occupied the less enviable seats on top. In the late 1880s, Herbert French, later of Boylston, was a stage coach driver on this very line. Notice those chapeaux!

By 1880, the B&M Railroad, Massachusetts Central Division, was running through Boylston with two scheduled stops. The first was at the South Clinton Station, which was located on the west side of Route 70 beyond Duffy Road. This 1896 picture shows a rather unpretentious depot with the stationmaster taking it easy out front. At the left is his horse and buggy, making this scene "hay burner vs. coal burner."

The second railway stop was at the Boylston Station located in the Sawyer's Mills section. The trains would stop for passengers and to load and unload freight. Taken a few years before the coming of the Wachusett Reservoir, the picture shows a somewhat better depot with signal lights and a platform.

In the summer months, the electric cars, like this one, were open. In 1910, George "Burt" Hazard of Boylston was a motorman on the trolleys. Here he is driving a car to Union Station in Worcester. Service like this allowed people to become more mobile and move to more rural areas yet maintain a connection to larger cities.

Burt Hazard was a motorman for the Worcester-Clinton Trolley Line. Here he is decked out in his uniform looking every inch the professional.

The motorman on the left is Burt Hazard Jr., *c.* 1910. It is said that he shot a deer in deer season from the trolley on which he was working, which just happened to be in Boylston!

On December 10, 1898, the Worcester & Clinton Electric Street Railway was officially opened. It serviced Morningdale and Boylston Center on its way to and from Worcester. To celebrate the occasion, a banquet with a sumptuous menu was held for town officials at the Clinton House.

Opening of Worcester & Clinton Electric Street Railway.

∴ MENU. ∴

BLUE POINTS.
Taragon.   Lemon.

HARE—American Style.
Celery.   Olives.

SPANISH MACKEREL.
Sliced Cucumbers.   Potatoes, Natural.

MALLARD DUCK.
Currant Jelly.   Mashed Potatoes.   Onions.   Squash.

Roman Punch.

QUAIL AU PAIN ROTI SEC.
Sliced Tomatoes.   Julienne Potatoes.   Dressed Lettuce.

Cigarettes.

ENGLISH PLUM PUDDING.
Brandy Sauce.

APPLE PIE.   SQUASH PIE.

FROZEN PUDDING.
Whipped Cream.

LADY FINGERS.   KISSES.   FRUIT.   NUTS.

COFFEE.   CIGARS.

CLINTON HOUSE.
J. S. RUSSELL & CO., PROPRIETORS.   SATURDAY, DEC. 10, 1898.

The Boylston Trolley Car Barn was located at the corner of French Drive and Route 70. This 1898 photo shows the building, plus a work car with trackmen aboard. Trolley service was discontinued in 1928 when buses were put into service.

The first German immigrants arrived here in 1865. George and Dora Kiesling came to Boylston 29 years later in 1894. George was employed by the textile plant at Sawyer's Mills. They eventually were able to purchase property on Duffy Road.

Luigi and Chiara Chiarelli were both from Italy and arrived in Boylston c. 1915. This photograph of them was taken in the 1960s. Many of their descendants still live in town and their family is considered the longest residing Italian-American family in Boylston. The influx of immigrants created a new kind of community with more ethnic and religious diversity.

Someone in Boylston owned this early Studebaker that was photographed in 1913. That owner must have been the topic of conversation at the Center Store and at the Ladies Aid meetings. Even the dog likes it!

George and Laura Dodge Boyden were leaving on their honeymoon in 1909. This looks like a Studebaker.

Six

ALL AROUND TOWN

This is a view taken in late fall 1886, looking north up Route 70 from the center. The trees are bare and forlorn. On the left is the original Center Store. Next to it is the Red Barn, and on the far right is the town hall.

This is a rare glimpse of the Boylston Public Library when it was located on the first floor of the town hall. The man is George L. Wright, who was the first librarian from 1880 to 1936. For the previous 92 years the town had relied on a private, members only, Social Library. As of 1880, the books were transferred to the public facility.

The town hall was built in 1830 with money given to the town by Ward Nicholas Boylston of Boston and Princeton. This c. 1900 photo shows how accurately the building was restored in the 1980s, up to and including a replica of the lamp over the front door. Incidentally, the structure on the right is not an addition but a commode!

The original Center Store was built in 1811 and was for over 100 years the commercial hub of Boylston center. Not only did Boylstonians go there for edibles and other household necessities, but also to pick up their mail and exchange the latest gossip. At this time (1905), the owner was George Hastings & Sons. The awnings add a nice touch.

This late 1930s view of the "new" Center Store also shows the Red Barn restaurant. Upon closer inspection, a gas pump and even a Mobil sign can be seen.

This is a great scene of the center in the 1890s. At left is the old schoolhouse, and to its right is the brick tavern. There was an abundance of shade trees, no electric wires, and no cars. If you wanted peace and quiet, this was the place to live.

This is the junction of Main and School Streets, looking south, as it appeared in 1894. The streets are packed dirt and are bordered by stately trees. The Old Burial Ground can be seen in the far distance. Imagine navigating this on a rainy spring day!

The Old Burial Ground pictured in 1904 was first used in 1743 for the burial of a young boy. It contains the remains of many of our earliest settlers and veterans of the Revolutionary War, including Captain Robert Andrews of Minuteman fame.

The Taylor Tavern was built in 1760 by David Taylor, and was an inn for 50 years. This 1886 photo shows an ivy-covered house that still stands opposite the Old Burial Ground.

The 1818 brick tavern was built by Silas Hastings. The ivy-covered inn was in operation until 1844. It has a magnificent second-story ballroom that was used in earlier days for all manners of social activities.

The elderly man, Azro Waterman, is shown here in 1900 resting by the watering trough that originally sat on a fieldstone base. Mr. Waterman was 83 years old when the picture was taken.

The Sawyer Memorial Library was built in 1904 and held 5,500 volumes when it first opened. Built of cobbled fieldstone, it continues to grace the common. It is ironic that Mr. Wright, the librarian at the time, wrote that in his opinion the building would prove to be too small in a short time. How prophetic he was!

This is a side view of the 1904 public library. The circular room in the center is quite unusual.

This 1886 view of Main Street is looking south. On the far right is the former ell of the Taylor Tavern, which was originally used as a country store. To its left is the Taylor Tavern.

At the left, on Central Street just down from the center, was the home of George L. Wright, town historian from 1880 to 1943. On the right was a shoe shop operated by Mr. Wright's father, Joseph Wright. This is an 1886 photo.

In 1886, James W. Woods owned this home at the crest of Cottonwood Place, overlooking the center. It had originally been built by Reverend Ward Cotton between 1800 and 1810. An earlier house, built in 1733, once stood almost opposite the present building.

This 1886 photo shows the house at 30 School Street, which was built in 1809 by Amasa Keyes. The ell of the house was used as a cobbler shop.

This is one of the last photos taken of Sawyer's Mills center before its demolition to make way for the construction of the reservoir. The bridge leads to the store and houses on the right side.

This view is of Mill Street, the main thoroughfare at Sawyer's Mills. This 1880s photo shows the textile mill on the left and the superintendent's house on the right. The children posing in the foreground add a delightful element to the scene.

The "old" store at Sawyer's Mills was photographed in 1880. It was built in 1862 and was owned and operated by a long list of storekeepers. None of the youngsters is identified.

This is an 1870s view of the second store in Sawyer's Mills. It was built in 1862 by the Lancaster Company. The first proprietor was Edgar Bruce & Co. The post office was located in the same building. The store was replaced in 1890 by a third building.

This photo of the residence of the superintendent of the textile mill at Sawyer's Mills was taken around 1886. It was built c. 1830 by Captain Eli Lamson and was eventually purchased by the Lancaster Mill Company as a home for the superintendent. The last man to occupy this position was J. Nelson Ball, who ironically worked on the 1870 addition to the mill building.

This is a late 1890s view of the rear of the Sawyer's Mills Store and of the iron bridge that spanned the Nashua River. Note the long and graceful piazza on the second floor.

This c. 1910 panoramic view of Morningdale village in Boylston was taken from the back of the house at 9 Miles Avenue, looking east. Main Street runs from left to right and Cook Street is at the far left. The houses depicted include, from left to right: 11 Cook Street, 32 Main Street, 25 Main Street (the three-story building at the corner of Cook), 18 Main Street, Flagg Street, 16 Main Street, and 14 Main Street.

George Glazier built a house in 1892 at 51 Main Street in Morningdale. Frederick Abbott occupied it for many years. Here is a 1910 photo showing Fred and his wife, Nellie, seated on the porch of their lovely home. After his death, the property was owned by Albert "Dutchy" Toombs, who had been Abbott's caretaker. He remained there until 1976.

The Morningdale Water District was legally formed in 1949 with Joseph Armstrong as the first superintendent. This photo shows the first successful drilling of their well off Route 70, dug by the R.H. White Company in 1948.

One of the most productive mills in the Morningdale section of town was the Bannister Mill. This 1905 photo shows the mill when Henry Seaver was the proprietor. This mill had a good supply of water from Sewall Pond. The Bannisters were accustomed to clear the brook of silt and rubbish by driving a pair of horses up the stream with a triangular plow.

Located in the southeast corner of Boylston, Straw Hollow received its name sometime before 1856 because the local inhabitants produced straw products during the winter months. This is a view of the Stearns house built around 1918. An earlier house on this site that burned had been the home of a prominent orchard keeper (William A. Moore), and of the creator of gourmet ice cream (Eubert Laws of Boston).

Diamond Hill received its name because of the diamond-like crystals found in the area. Near the top of that hill is the Herbert A. Brigham home, photographed in 1930. The house was built around 1812 by Ozias Partridge. Later, six members of the Brigham family owned and occupied the house. This interior scene shows a fireplace with antique accouterments.

At the top of Pulpit Hill (off Scar Hill Road) is the Africans' House, so-called because several African-American families lived there, including John Richardson and George Hazard. It was built in the 1850s by L.L. Flagg. Flagg purchased two old shops, transported them to this site, and joined them into a single dwelling.

Seven

NOSES TO THE GRINDSTONE

This panoramic view of the Sawyer's Mills complex shows not only the factory building but also the surrounding stores and homes. Tenement houses were built by the company and rented to the mill workers. Originally settled c. 1728 by Joseph Sawyer, by 1737 it contained a blacksmith shop, a sawmill, and a fulling mill.

A winter scene shows Sawyer's Mills and the adjacent area in great detail. Taken around 1895, it shows on the far left the row houses built by the company to house workers. The road in the upper portion led from Boylston Center to the mill. The bridge in the lower right is a railroad trestle. The mill employed about 125 people, mostly women.

The largest industrial venture in Boylston was Sawyer's Mills. This 1896 photo shows the Lancaster Mill building, which annually produced over 1 million pounds of gingham yarn. The Nashua River flows by the building, which housed 90 spinning frames. The Lancaster Mill Corporation bought the complex in 1862.

This is a modern view of the remains of Bannister Mills, which was located in the Morningdale section of town.

This late 1890s photo shows the Bannister Mill on Mill Road. Built around 1812 by Nathan Bannister, it housed both a gristmill and a lumber mill. Sewall Brook provided the waterpower.

...for some time and had its post office in this house.

A French Canadian named Terullius Roy built a box mill on Scar Hill Road around 1860. He manufactured wooden shoeboxes. He eventually ran a sawmill to provide his own lumber and eliminate an added expense. The original mill burned, and the one pictured is of a later vintage; however, the barn in the background was built by Mr. Roy.

Asa Bee took over the Roy Mill around 1875 and rebuilt the business. The house in the background had been built by Mr. Roy. The mill continued to produce wooden boxes.

In the mid-1880s, George Hazard reopened the Howe brickyard on Route 70 north of the center. The clay used to manufacture the bricks was taken from a pit on the opposite side of the street. Hazard's bricks were used to build factories and homes in the area. He imported a number of French-Canadian brickmakers whose work he admired. This 1890 photo shows one of the buildings and lines of bricks drying.

This is another view of Hazard's Brickyard. Some of the laborers are carrying the forms used to mold the bricks. It is possible that it is Mr. Hazard astride the horse at the far left. The building looks as if it would fall apart if a good gust of wind hit it.

This is a 1920s photo of what was known as the Austin Nelson house. The house was built around 1834 and located on Stiles Road near Harbor Brook, though it was gone by 1963. It was once occupied by a man who sold fish from a wagon door-to-door, probably in the late 1890s. There were scores of small business ventures during the 19th and early 20th century.

This building was erected c. 1821 by Squire Aaron White and was located between the present Congregational Church parsonage and the church itself. White originally used it as a store, until 1846. It was later moved to Main Street (north) and converted into a dwelling. The center post office was located there for a short time in the 1850s.

The Winchester Blacksmith Shop on Central Street was photographed in 1910. Tradition has it that Mr. Winchester used "salty" language while working. Mothers who took their children out for a stroll blocked their ears as they walked by the shop.

This *c*. 1912 photo shows the blacksmith shop that was located just next to 19 Central Street, heading toward Northboro. There had been a shop there as early as 1800. It was still operating well into the 1920s. The building is plastered with ads for Buffalo Bill Cody's Wild West Show. (This photo is reproduced by permission of The Huntington Library, San Marino, California.)

The Model Dairy has been a town fixture for more than 70 years. Here is the founder, Robert Wentzell, in a 1938–39 photo, standing next to his delivery truck. (R. Wentzell photo.)

This is an early 1930s photo of a Model Dairy truck. The milk was advertised as "Grade A" and "Tuberculin Tested." (R. Wentzell photo.)

Two Model Dairy trucks appear in this 1940s photo taken in front of the dairy building on Sewall Street. Robert's son Roger took over the business and both he and his truck have become part of Boylston's landscape. (R. Wentzell photo.)

W. RES. · BOYLSTON
EAST TOWARDS DUMPING PLATFORM 22 SEC. 8
APR 24 1902

A 1902 photo shows the basin of the Wachusett Reservoir being prepared for inundation by immigrant laborers. Vegetation is being removed and carted away. The structure in the right center was a dumping platform.

Eight

WHAT DO YOU RAISE BESIDES ROCKS?

This unidentified farmer proudly shows off his prize oxen, which are pulling a loaded hayrick. This mode of transport predated John Deere's tractors.

Taken c. 1910, the photo shows Herbert A. Brigham driving a milk wagon. The boy and the dog are not identified.

This turn-of-the-century photo exemplifies the agricultural nature of the town. Leading the team of oxen pulling the hay wagon is John Lundgren, who was a farmhand on Miss Jennie Flagg's farm off Route 140.

The farm of Montraville Flagg was one of the finest in Boylston. This c. 1890 photo shows a field of corn with the home in the background. The Flaggs named the place "Elmwood Farm," a name that is still used today. Montraville Flagg is in the cornfield. In the front are, from left to right, Richard A. Flagg, Alice Tilton, and Monson Flagg.

In this 1903 photo taken at Levi Lincoln Flagg's farm, four young women seem to be enjoying their wagon ride.

This turn-of-the-century photo was taken on the Brigham Farm on Ball Hill. The place had been in the Brigham family since 1834. Nobody going on this hayride is identified.

The Phineas Howe house was built c. 1730 and its owners cultivated the land for 150 years. Taken in 1886, the photo is made striking by the lack of trees in the background. The barns housed all forms of farm animals. It was later owned by George Hazard, who ran a brickyard off Route 70.

James Longley built his home on Rocky Pond Road in 1784. His 300-acre farm was one of the most productive of its time. Longley was the first to use a metal plow in Boylston and the first to graft apple trees. Two prize bulls are pictured in the center of this 1886 photo. The house is still standing today, a fine example of Georgian architecture.

This barn was part of the holdings of Lyman and Edward Walker and was located on Linden Street. A good portion of it was being used by the Mount Pleasant Country Club until 1998.

This imposing creature belonged to John Flagg of Diamond Hill Road and by the looks of him, he was king of the pasture, and certainly a lot of bull.

Nine

SAINTS, SINNERS, AND PEOPLE IN BETWEEN

This portrait of Mrs. John B. Gough's nieces and nephews was taken in the 1870s. Pictured are, from left to right, the following: (front row) Anna Whitcomb, Nellie Whitcomb, Mrs. Catherine Gough, and Fanny Whitcomb; (back row) Walter Whitcomb and Herbert D. Gough.

Ward Nicholas Boylston (1744–1828) was a member of the financially successful Boston Boylstons. The town was named for this family in 1786. Ward gave the town a sum of money with which to build a town hall. This portrait by Gilbert Charles Stuart hangs in the Harvard Club in Boston. The silk dressing gown and pompadour wig are nice touches.

The first minister of the Boylston church was Reverend Dr. Ebenezer Morse (1718–1802). Harvard-educated, he took on the new church in 1743 and remained here until he was dismissed in 1775. He was an outspoken Tory and opposed some of the more popular Revolutionary principles. He was banned from his pulpit but continued to call himself the "pastor of the Boylston church."

John Bartholomew Gough (1817–1886) came to this country when he was just a boy and drifted into a life of alcoholism. In 1842 he took the pledge of total abstinence and started a new life. He became an overnight sensation as a lecturer and was soon in great demand all over America, Canada, England, Scotland, and Ireland. He became a leader in the Temperance movement.

Mary (Whitcomb) Gough (1819–1890), wife of the famous temperance lecturer John B. Gough, was a teacher. She married Gough in 1843 and became his soul mate and constant companion. She was the mistress of Hillside, Gough's estate, and managed a large household including young nieces and nephews who lived with her. She created a haven of peace for her husband, who saw her as his strength.

In 1848, John B. Gough built a beautiful mansion house in the Morningdale section of Boylston. This 1890 photo shows the house at the height of its elegance. It was considered by many to be one of the three most beautiful homes in Massachusetts.

This photo shows the living room in the Gough house looking into the sunroom. The décor is typical Victorian with numerous green plants and stuffed birds adorning the walls. The portrait of Gough now stands in the Boylston Museum.

This is a view through the Gough library looking into what he called the library annex that handled the overflow of books. Note the lace doily on the back of the chair. It was customary at the time to cover chairs with antimacassars such as these.

This photo of the library in the John Gough house was taken c. 1880. Mr. Gough collected 3,000 volumes, many beautifully bound in fine leather.

Sara Hartshorn Partridge (1811–1890) was the second wife of Deacon Simeon Partridge, and the stepmother of John W. Partridge, who fought and died in the Civil War. She and several family members and friends went to the cemetery to decorate the graves of the soldiers who were buried there. She is considered the founder of Memorial Day in Boylston.

Mary (Avery) White (1778–1860), prolific diarist and correspondent, was the wife of one of Boylston's most successful men, Aaron White. However, her greatness lay in her ability to capture the flavor and trends of the time on paper. The Boylston Historical Society has copies of many of her letters that have been used in a book about her. She was active in the Abolitionist movement, Temperance, and the Missionary Society.

Levi Lincoln Flagg (1818–1907) was considered one of the town's wealthiest residents. He was a successful farmer and entrepreneur who owned property here and in Worcester. He operated a wholesale and retail slaughtering business and sold meat from wagons in surrounding towns. He was also a selectman, assessor, and town treasurer. When he died, he had amassed a fortune valued at $100,000.

Alexander Van Rensselaer Prouty (1828–1892) came here from North Brookfield. When he became interested in an older widow, his father wrote him to beware of this "creature" who was "spinning a web to entice him." Well he did not heed his father's advice and married Elizabeth Coolidge Hastings and lived happily ever after.

This charming 1864 photo of two girls surrounded by dolls was taken at the Congregational Church fair. The youngster at the right is Cora Benson, who was ten years old at the time. The other girl is not identified.

These are the "Busy Bees" whose origin and purpose are unknown. This *c.* 1908 photo shows seven young lasses in their Sunday best, looking quite demure and coy. The only identified young woman is Maude Hazard, on the far left.

George A. Flagg (1855–19??) carried on a lucrative cattle and slaughtering business. He also dealt in real estate and ran a large cider mill. In 1907, he was accused of setting fire to two tenement buildings he owned on Scar Hill Road. "Fire Bug Flagg," as he was called in the newspapers, was confined for a time to the State Mental Hospital in Worcester.

When the town celebrated its centennial in 1886, it chose the leading men in the community to organize the celebrations. Most were former selectmen. Others had served as assessors, treasurers, and school committee members. They were considered at the time to be the "Six Notables" of Boylston. Shown here are, from left to right, the following: (seated) Nathaniel Kendall and Elmer Shaw; (back row) Lyman Kendall, William Andrews, John Warner, and Albert Andrews.

Reverend Dr. Andrew Bigelow (1809–1882) was born in Boylston and became pastor of the local church in 1866. In 1880 he discovered gold off Linden Street, and in partnership with several financiers, began mining. Unfortunately it was a low grade ore and yielded no significant amount of money. On Sunday afternoons, people came from all over the county to gaze into the open mine shaft.

Mary (Andrews) French (1863–1949) was Boylston-born and bred. She was the town's first public school music teacher. In 1904, she became the town's telephone operator when there were only 75 telephones in operation. She conducted the telephone service at her Scar Hill Road home for 33 years. In 1937, the dial system was introduced, and the job of a switchboard operator became obsolete.

Fanny Maria Whitcomb (b. 1856), niece of Mrs. Mary Gough, became a teacher in the Boylston schools. In 1882, she became the first woman elected to the Boylston School Committee. In 1885, she became chairperson of that committee. She remained at Hillside until after Mrs. Gough's death.

Members of the Women's Christian Temperance Union were photographed in 1923. The local branch of the movement was born in the mid-19th century, and strong leadership was provided by the women of the community. This most intimidating group of reformers includes, from left to right, the following: (front row) Martha Warner, 86; Anna Tucker, 81; Henrietta Andrews, 87; and Hattie Walker, 81; (back row) Alma Boyden, Mary Knox, and Jeanette Devoe.

The first Boy Scout troop in Boylston was formed in 1919 by Colonel William Keck, who also became the first scoutmaster. This early 1920s photo shows the boys in their uniforms, which bear a striking resemblance to the U.S. Army World War I uniforms. Colonel Keck is the man second from the right. They even had a bugle boy!

Boylston's Girl Scout troop was founded in 1922 by Ruth L. Boyden. These girls, resplendent in their uniforms, were photographed a few years later at the town hall. Shown here are, from left to right, Grace Boyden, Alva Kinnear, Alice Donaldson, Doris Durrell, Ruth Stewart, Jean Tiemeyer, Alma Boyden, Ruth Harvey, Eunice Manning, Elizabeth Brigham, and Grace Hedlund.

George Lawson Wright (1856–1943) was one of Boylston's most prolific historians. He was also devoted to public service, and from 1884 to 1943 he served in practically every town office. He researched every aspect of town history and genealogy and was an amateur artist and calligrapher. Although much of his work was lost after his death, enough was salvaged to form the basis for the historical society's present collection.

Many may argue that this woman, Goldie Elizabeth Prouty (1896–19??) is the very apotheosis of the prim and proper turn-of-the-century young lady in this c. 1914 photo. She is seated at the piano with interesting sheet music to her left and right.

Here is Goldie in a somewhat more risque pose. Goldie later married George Benson and was an active member of many Boylston activities.

Ten

SABBATH MEMORIES

A lively spiritual life has always been a part of Boylston's history. Four Congregational churches have served the local people since 1743. This 1904 photo shows the Third Congregational Church atop the new common.

This *c.* 1885 photo shows the Third Congregational Church minus its steeple, which had been destroyed during a severe windstorm. It was replaced, but according to some members of the congregation, the newer version was not as graceful as the original.

The Fourth Congregational Church looks majestic in this winter scene taken in the mid-20th century. The church has had 23 pastors beginning in 1743. It celebrated its 250th anniversary in 1993.

The Reverend Israel Ainsworth was pastor of the local church from 1884 to 1887. A native of England, he came here from Boston, New Hampshire, and was a popular minister.

The so-called Bigelow Parsonage was built in 1873 by Reverend Andrew Bigelow, and served for many years as the residence of Boylston's ministers. It is located on Scar Hill Road and is a fine example of Mansard architecture.

The interior of the Third Congregational Church was photographed in 1901. It is decorated in mourning in honor of President McKinley, who had been assassinated. It was built in 1835.

A c. 1900 photo shows the interior of the Third Congregational Church. On the right is a fine pipe organ and in the center an ornately carved pulpit and chairs.

This 1921 photo is a side view of the Third Congregational Church, which burned in February 1924. The first church was built in 1743 on what is now called the old common.

The Third Congregational Church is shown burning in February 1924. The fire started in the basement and spread quickly to the upper floor of the 89-year-old structure. The efforts of fire fighters from Worcester and Clinton were in vain.

Sacred Heart Chapel opened on Palm Sunday, 1890. It accommodated 125 people and was serviced by priests from West Boylston. It was abandoned in 1900 and covered by the waters of the Wachusett Reservoir.

By 1890, the number of Catholics in Boylston, especially in the Sawyer's Mills area, had increased significantly. Church authorities allowed the building of the Sacred Heart Chapel in Sawyer's Mills.

The beautiful Morningdale Chapel was dedicated in 1913. The faithful in that section of town found it difficult to attend services in the center, so this chapel was erected. The local Congregational Church assumed the spiritual direction of this new place of worship. Its service to the community ended several decades ago.

St. Mary of the Hills Catholic Church was built in 1926 in the Morningdale section. It was a Mission chapel until 1952, when it was made a parish. A new and larger church replaced it in 1992 on Cross Street. (Fred Brown photo.)

The interior of St. Mary's is decorated for Easter. The charm of this small church lay in its very smallness, which lent itself to quiet prayer and contemplation. (Mary Hehir photo.)

In June 1961, Maureen Hehir made her First Communion at St. Mary's. She is pictured here in front of the Mary Shrine with Rev. Michael Shea, who served as pastor from 1954 to 1964. (Mary Hehir photo.)

www.ingramcontent.com/pod-product-compliance
Lightning Source LLC
Chambersburg PA
CBHW080851100426
42812CB00007B/1985